STORIES FROM ANCIENT CIVILISATIONS

Rome

For Sophia Giles Macmillan - S.H

Published by Evans Brothers Limited
2A Portman Mansions
Chiltern Street
London W1U 6NR

© Evans Brothers Limited 2004
First published 2004
Printed in China

British Library Cataloguing in Publication Data

Husain, Shahrukh
   Stories from Ancient Civilisations: Rome - (Stories
   from ancient civilisations)
   1. Mythology, Rome - Juvenile literature
   2. Rome - Civilization - Juvenile literature
   I.Title
   398.2'0937

ISBN 0 237 52445 7

CREDITS
Series Editor: Louise John
Editor: Julia Bird
Design: Robert Walster
Artworks: Bee Willey
Production: Jenny Mulvanny

STORIES FROM ANCIENT CIVILISATIONS

Rome

Shahrukh Husain
and Bee Willey

Evans

Introduction

Myths are probably the earliest stories ever told. People in ancient times used them to explain all that was important in life – how the universe was created, how the stars, sun, moon and planets appeared in the sky. To them, these elements were gods whom they worshipped and whom they believed controlled their lives. They wanted to keep the gods happy to gain their blessings.

Myths are often concerned with important rites of passage, such as birth, death and the afterlife and tend to have a moral. The story of Aeneas's visit to the Underworld tells us the ancient Romans believed people go to the Underworld after dying, where those who have lived honestly will go to the Elysian Fields and be happy. The same myth also tells us the importance of rituals in ancient Rome, for we learn that the souls of those who died without proper burials wandered endlessly in search of peace.

The Romans were a war-like nation, fighting against neighbouring tribes and eventually going on to conquer and rule an enormous part of the world. That is why their myths are about soldier heroes, brave deeds achieved for the good of the country, the building of cities and the conquest of lands. The Roman invaders took their gods and myths with them on their travels. As they settled somewhere new, an exchange took place. They introduced the Roman gods to the local people and in turn began to worship some of theirs. So more myths were added and old stories blended with new ones. Sometimes the same gods were called different names by different cultures. This is particularly true of the Roman and Greek gods, where the Roman gods like Jupiter, Venus and Mars were known as Zeus, Aphrodite and Ares in Greek mythology.

The Romans strongly believed that the gods helped and guided their actions. They made sacrifices like Aeneas did to reach the Underworld and organised rituals like Numa Pompilius did before important events to make sure the gods approved. Each Roman clan had its own special family god or goddess known as a tutelary deity. Roman rulers liked to claim descent from the gods. The great emperor Julius Caesar erected temples and statues to Venus and Mars during his rule, claiming they were his ancestors.

Most Roman myths come from the work of the Roman historian Livy (59 BCE-17 CE), who wrote them as if they were real stories from history. For a long time they were taken to be true accounts and showed the Roman kings as they wanted to be seen – as sons of the gods with the divine right to rule.

Contents

The Voyages of Aeneas

This story is taken from the Aeneid, an epic tale written by Virgil, one of ancient Rome's greatest writers. It tells of the voyages of Aeneas, a Trojan prince, after the fall of Troy and describes the first settlement of Rome. The Aeneid also claims Aeneas was the son of the goddess Venus, which made him a born leader and a worthy forefather of Rome.

TROY WAS BURNING. Aeneas knew he had to leave. He had fought courageously to save it, now it was time to find a new home. His father Anchises was too weak to walk, so Aeneas hoisted him on to his back and set off for the outskirts of the city where other Trojan refugees were waiting.

'Lead the way,' they said. 'We will follow.'
They set sail from the port, and soon landed in Thrace.

'Let us rest here. I will light a fire to make an offering to the gods,' said Aeneas. He snapped off a branch from a nearby bush. Instantly, a large drop of blood appeared where the branch had broken.

'Aeneas, brother, spare me,' a voice said. 'I am a prince of Troy. I was sent to Thrace to be protected by the king. Instead, he killed me for my wealth and buried me here under this bush.'

Aeneas was horrified. 'The king's treachery has made the soil of Thrace unclean,' he said to his followers. 'We cannot stay here.'

They journeyed on. In Crete the Trojans planted crops. But the crops failed and the Trojans became sick. So Aeneas and his men sailed on until they came to an island which appeared deserted except for herds of cows.

'At last,' Aeneas rejoiced, 'we've found our new home.'

The men slaughtered some cows and prepared a great feast.

'Let us give thanks for our fortune,' Aeneas began. But a swarm of monstrous creatures swooped down and snatched the food from their hands. Furious, the hungry men struck out at the huge birds, who had faces like pale, hungry women.

'We are the Harpies,' shrieked their leader. 'We will make your lives miserable because you have killed our animals and attacked us.'

Aeneas and his men decided to sail on to look for the nearby land of Hesperia. As they voyaged towards it, the sky darkened and the winds rose, whipping the water into huge waves. Some boats crashed against the rocks, casting men out into the sea and Aeneas fell to his knees in despair, begging the gods for mercy.

Neptune, god of the sea, took pity on the Trojans.

'Cease your destruction!' he commanded the winds. Then he told the creatures of the sea to repair the Trojan boats and set them safely on their course.

At last, exhausted, the Trojans arrived in Hesperia.

'Come, father,' Aeneas said to Anchises, 'let us step together on to the land where the gods have sent us.'

Anchises did not reply.

'Father?' Aeneas said again. But Anchises had died during the storm. Heartbroken, Aeneas told his men he had to find a Sibyl – a prophetess with the power to reunite him with his father. People told him that the Sibyl of Cumae was very wise and powerful. Aeneas searched everywhere until, eventually, he found her cave.

'Take me to the world of the dead,' he pleaded. 'I must say goodbye to my father.'

'It is dangerous but I will take you,' the Sibyl replied. 'First, seek out the golden bough, which grows on a tree in the sacred wood. If you are meant to go to the Underworld, it will come away easily when you grasp it.'

Aeneas stood in the woods, looking around him. Where should he begin? Above him a pair of doves began cooing. Aeneas's spirits lifted. Doves were the favourite birds of the goddess Venus, his mother. The doves flew ahead and he followed until they landed on a small tree. Aeneas looked among its leaves carefully. There he saw, glowing in the darkness, exactly what he was looking for.

'Help me, mother,' he breathed, closing his eyes as he grasped the golden bough. Immediately, it came away and was replaced by another.

He hurried back to the Sibyl.

'Think carefully, Aeneas,' she warned him. 'It is very hard to enter the world of the dead, and to return to Earth is almost impossible.'

'I must see my father this last time,' Aeneas insisted.

The Sibyl told Aeneas to make an offering to Proserpina, Queen of the Dead, over a sacrificial fire which sizzled and leapt. A mighty roar broke the silence in the Sibyl's smoky cave and was followed by the furious barking of dogs.

'The gods have heard us!' exclaimed the Sibyl. 'It is time. Be brave.'

Aeneas felt himself plunging below ground. Flimsy creatures beat against his face. They were the evil beings that made living hard: Hate, Anger, Sickness and Toil. Down, down Aeneas went with the Sibyl, until they stopped on the shores of a black river beside a boat. People thronged around it, but Charon, the ferryman, turned many of them away.

'Why is he turning them away?' Aeneas asked.

'They did not receive proper burials,' the Sibyl replied. 'They will wander the Underworld until their time comes.'

The Sibyl approached Charon, holding out the golden bough. 'Aeneas has brought this gift for your queen.'

Charon ushered Aeneas and the Sibyl on to his ferry. After a long, harsh journey, they arrived at a forked road.

'One branch leads to Elysium, the home of the blessed,' the Sibyl said. 'Let's hope we take it.'

They chose a path. Immediately, they were surrounded by lush fields and clear, tinkling streams.

'I'm sure my father is here,' Aeneas said joyfully.

The Romans believed that the souls of the dead went to the Underworld. According to Virgil, the soul was made of fire, water, earth and air. Humans were less pure than the gods because they contained more earth. In the Underworld, they were purified in fire, water or air before being reborn. Evil people returned to Earth as savage animals. Noble people stayed forever in a beautiful part of the Underworld known as Elysium or the Elysian Fields.

'I've been waiting for you,' Anchises's voice replied. He embraced his son. 'Continue your journey,' he told Aeneas. 'It will end by the mouth of the River Tiber. There you will create a country which will one day become the greatest in the world.'

With Anchises's words ringing in his ears, Aeneas returned to his men and they continued their voyage until at last they arrived at the Tiber. As they landed, Aeneas sent a message to King Latinus, the ruler of the land, to say that they came in peace.

Latinus called his advisors. 'The diviners say my daughter Lavinia will marry a man from foreign lands who will rule my country. I believe Aeneas is that man.'

'Aeneas's fame has spread far and wide,' replied the king's advisors. 'His mother is Venus and Neptune protects him. He is worthy of our princess.'

King Latinus walked down to welcome Aeneas and offer him Lavinia's hand in marriage. At last, Aeneas had led the Trojans to their journey's end. They built a city and named it Lavinium after Aeneas's bride. In time, Rome was built there and the Roman empire flourished and grew, just as Anchises had promised.

The Sibyl of Cumae

This story is about the Roman custom of consulting oracles. The Sibyl of Cumae was one of the most famous oracles or prophetesses. Her name was Herophile and the god Apollo made her life last as many years as the number of grains of sand she could hold in one hand.

KING TARQUINUS THE SECOND LOOKED SCORNFULLY AT THE NINE BUNDLES THE OLD WOMAN HELD OUT. She called them books, but they were really bundles of dried leaves. She said they were prophecies but for all he knew they were just the ramblings of a mad woman.

'The price is outrageous,' he said. 'I am not interested in far-fetched prophecies.'

'If King Tarquinus, the protector of Rome, is not interested I will burn them,' the woman replied.

'Isn't it better to sell them for less than burn them?'

The woman shook her head. 'Better they burn than go to a man who does not value them or Rome's future.'

The old woman was a wise and famous Sibyl who had lived for nine hundred and ninety years in a cave in

Cumae. Every time she predicted future events, she wrote them on leaves and left them at the mouth of her cave. Sometimes people collected the precious leaves but others scattered and were lost.

The Sybil carefully placed three of the books on the ground and set them alight.

Tarquinus could not believe his eyes. He had heard about this Sibyl like everyone else. She had predicted that Aeneas would arrive on these shores and build a city. She had even foreseen the building of Rome. Who knew what great secrets of the future were held in those pages?

The Sibylline Prophecies bought by Tarquinus Priscus Lucas, the fifth king of Rome (616-579 BCE) remained in Jupiter's temple until 83 BCE when the temple was burned down. The prophecies that survived were last consulted in 636 CE.

Tarquinus stepped forward, holding up his hand as the Sibyl lifted three more books to fling on the fire. 'Enough!' he commanded. 'You have proved your point. I will buy the remaining books. How much do you want now?'

'The price remains the same,' replied the Sibyl. 'Take it or leave it.'

'I will not give in to you,' Tarquinus said angrily. 'Burn your prophecies.'

'Since you weigh the future in money,' the Sibyl said, 'it is better that I do.'

She swooped to the ground and set three more books alight.

Tarquinus could take no more. 'I will buy the other three for the price of all nine!'

The Sibyl handed the books to Tarquinus. 'Keep them safe and consult them in hard times and in times of confusion. I will not be here much longer but my words will guide you. You have judged well.'

Tarquinus placed the books in the temple of Jupiter where they would be tended by priests and consulted for advice when needed.

The Sibyl returned home. She was expecting a letter. She turned it over and looked at the seal which was made from the earth of Erythrae, her home. The feel and sight of her country's soil after hundreds of years warmed the Sibyl's heart.

'At last,' she thought, 'I can die in peace.'

She had done Rome an immense service. She had left behind her prophecies to guide it to greater and greater glory in the years to come.

Romulus and Remus

This story is about the godly beginnings of Rome's rulers, Romulus and Remus. With Mars as their ancestor, the descendants of Romulus and Remus could claim great power and the right to be king. The story also mentions Vesta, goddess of the home, whose fire burned day and night in the Forum in Rome. The Forum was the centre of religion, business and politics in the city.

The Vestal virgins who served in Vesta's temple inside the Forum were selected from important families and carefully trained for their duties. These were to tend the eternal fires of Vesta and to mix the offerings of grains for public ceremonies.

The Sons of Rea Silva

REA SILVA WAS THE DAUGHTER OF KING NUMITOR OF ALBA LONGA. Her uncle Amulius had snatched the throne from her father and exiled him to the countryside. It made her furious to think that her father, betrayed by his own brother, was wandering helplessly somewhere. She wanted to pay Amulius back by having a son who would win back the kingdom. But Amulius intended to stop her.

'I am going to honour you,' Amulius told her, 'by making you a Vestal virgin. You will dedicate your life to serving at the goddess Vesta's shrine.'

Rea's plan was shattered. The Vestal virgins did not marry for many years, so she would never be able to have sons. Still, she accepted. If she refused, she would be killed and then there would be no one to help her father.

Rea worked hard at the shrine of the goddess and, each day, asked the gods to help her. Then, one morning when she was out in the woods collecting water for the temple, a huge, glowing figure appeared in front of her.

'Do you know who I am?' the figure asked.

'You must be a god,' she replied, falling to her knees.

'I am Mars,' replied the figure. 'Go in peace and continue to serve Vesta. I shall grant your prayers.'

Rea told no one about her meeting with Mars but as she went about her daily duties, she often wondered what he could have meant. She knew that the only way she could help her father was by having a son and that just

wasn't possible while she served at the temple.

One morning, she found the answer to her question. Two beautiful baby boys lay gurgling beside her when she woke. Mars had sent her two sons who would have the power to restore the throne to her father.

'I must hide them,' Rea thought in a panic. 'The priests will never believe the boys were a gift from Mars. They will kill me or expel me from the temple.'

Just then, the door to her chamber burst open with a bang. Three soldiers marched in.

'Take the children!' commanded the captain. The others lunged forward. Rea clutched her babies, crouching to protect them with her body. One soldier dragged her away while the other grabbed the infants.

'Throw them into the Tiber,' the captain commanded.

'Let me take them far away where we are strangers,' Rea begged. 'I promise they'll never be seen in Alba Longa again.'

The captain and his men took the infants and walked out without another word. Rea fell to her knees, crying out to Mars to save her sons.

'Your Majesty,' the captain reported to Amulius. 'Rea Silva's boys are at

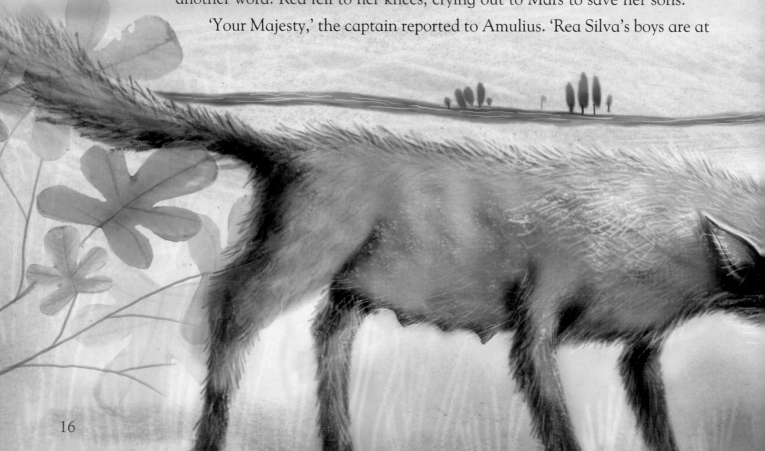

this very moment on their way to the Tiber to be fed to the waters.'

Amulius laughed loudly. 'The river is in flood,' he bellowed. 'They will drown at once!'

The Tiber was indeed in flood. Its water whirled and gushed right up to the highest boundary, then ebbed, leaving shimmering pools behind on the river's banks. The soldiers saw the waters swell and burst their banks, then rise, spiralling upwards. Quickly they threw the little boys into the waves and fled. The babies floated on the water as it gushed over a mound of sand at the base of a fig tree. But as the floods retreated, their little bodies were left resting on the mound. Miraculously, the floods had worked in their favour.

At dawn, a she-wolf wandered down to the water's edge looking for something to feed her cubs. Her sharp eyes picked out a movement at the foot of the fig tree. Her keen nose sniffed out the scent of flesh. Slowly, carefully, she edged her way to the twin boys. Then, just as she

reached them, they began to cry. The she-wolf sensed that these infants were hungry for food and comfort, just like her own cubs.

Suddenly, her hunting instincts disappeared. She lay down beside the baby boys, encircled them with her furry body and began suckling them. When they had fallen asleep, she stayed awhile, giving warmth to their tiny bodies. Soon the king's herdsman Faustulus would let loose the royal herds and flocks to graze in the nearby pastures. The she-wolf would find a suitable catch for her cubs then.

Faustulus let his eyes wander as he approached the pastures. He loved this time of morning when all was quiet and the world of men was mostly asleep. His eyes came to rest on the fig tree and he saw the she-wolf curled around the infants. He raced up to the tree as the she-wolf gently detached herself and loped away.

Faustulus fell to his knees and examined the babies. They were warm and healthy. Their small bodies bore no sign of any scratches or bites. Faustulus lifted the babies, looking into their faces.

'Praise the gods,' he cried out. 'That she-wolf has been feeding them. Her milk is still on their lips.'

Leaving the king's animals to graze peacefully, he hurried home to his wife, holding the twin boys close to his chest.

'Larentia,' he called. 'I saw a miracle today!'

Larentia took the babies from her husband and cradled them gently in her arms.

'The gods have sent us two sons,' she whispered. 'Their names will be Romulus and Remus.'

And so Rea Silva's sons were safe.

In ancient times, there was a hut on the Palatine Hill that people believed to be the home of Faustulus and Larentia. When Faustulus died, he was buried in the Forum in Rome. Later, his tomb was decorated with a lion sculpture to honour him.

The Foundation of Rome

This story is found in Books From the Foundation of the City by the famous Roman historian, Livy (59 BCE - 17 CE). It describes how Romulus eventually discovered his true origins and became the rightful founder and first ruler of the city of Rome.

Rome was built across seven hills. The Aventine Hill, overlooking the River Tiber, is in the far south of where Rome is now. The Capitoline Hill, also known as the Aix, is the smallest of the hills, and the Palatine, where the kings' palaces were later built, was the most important.

LUPERCALIA, THE SPRING FESTIVAL, WAS COMING SOON. Romulus and Remus were looking forward to it and so were all their friends. Prayers would be offered to please the god and goddess of nature, Faunus and Fauna, so that the fields and valleys around the Palatine Hill would be fertile again this year. There would be fun and games for everyone.

Romulus and Remus were much admired. They were the strongest young men in the region, the fastest runners, the most agile athletes. All the other young men wanted to be like them. Their parents, Faustulus and Larentia, were very proud of them. The boys had brought them good luck. Since their arrival, Faustulus and Larentia's family had been happier, healthier and wealthier.

The young men were preparing for the festival. Romulus stood at the starting point, ready to run his race while his father watched. Some distance away, Remus showed off his enormous strength. He completed the final test and walked from the ring, amid cheers, to where Larentia stood watching.

Above the cheers, Remus heard a voice calling. 'Remus! Help me, Remus! Bandits have stolen my cattle.'

Immediately, Remus ran to help. He followed the cattle tracks until he came to a remote area. Darkness was falling but Remus knew his way well. The sound of lowing told him the herd was nearby. Remus flexed his muscles and crept silently towards it. The next moment, he was surrounded by bandits.

'This is the end of you,' growled the thugs. 'We are taking you to the owner of these lands to be put to death.'

'Huh!' snorted Remus. 'Why should he kill me for chasing criminals?'

'You and your brother have troubled us for years,' snarled the leader, ordering his men to gag Remus. 'Now we will have our revenge.'

They bound Remus's hands and marched him to the landowner.

'My lord,' said the bandit leader. 'This man and his brother make regular raids on your lands. They deserve to be severely punished.'

'Put him to death,' commanded the landowner. Remus tried to explain that he and his brother raided only the hiding places of the bandits who lurked in the area. But the landowner would not listen.

Back on the Palatine Hill, a messenger brought Romulus the news that Remus had been condemned to death.

'Go to him immediately,' Faustulus ordered.

Romulus was surprised. 'Isn't it better to make a rescue plan?'

Faustulus shook his head. 'The landowner Numitor is your grandfather.' Faustulus then told Romulus the whole story – how Amulius had stolen the throne from his brother Numitor and had Rea Silva's sons thrown to the floods. 'That is when I found you,' he said, 'suckling on a she-wolf. When I discovered who you were, I said nothing in case Amulius tried to kill you. But now it is time to tell the world who you really are.'

Romulus said goodbye to his parents and went straight to Numitor. 'Remus and I are your grandsons,' he told him. 'We will fight King Amulius and win back your throne.'

Numitor could hardly believe his luck. Together with his grandsons, he defeated the evil Amulius and freed their mother, Rea Silva. Numitor's family

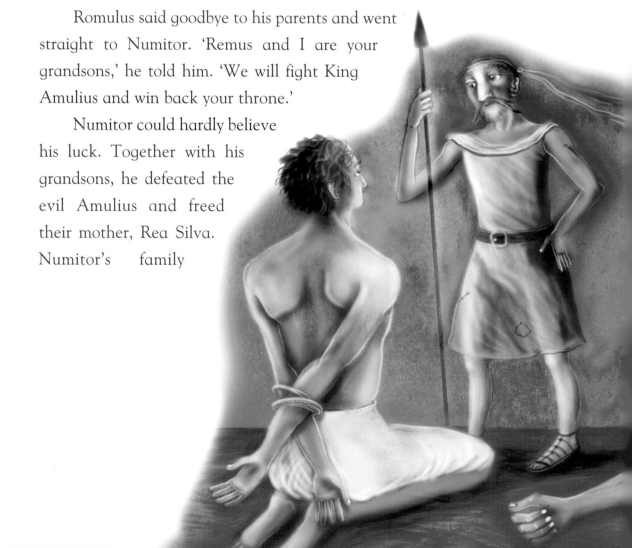

was together again. As they helped their grandfather rebuild his kingdom, Romulus looked around him and saw that their homeland was becoming crowded.

'I shall build a new city,' he declared, 'on the banks of the Tiber where Faustulus found me.'

'I was there, too,' said Remus. 'I should build it.'

The twins turned to Numitor and Rea Silva.

'The older brother has first choice,' said Numitor.

'But they are the same age,' Rea replied.

'Then we must ask the gods to help,' Numitor decided.

So Romulus went to the Palatine Hill and Remus went to the Aventine. Each brother prayed to the god of that place to send him a sign saying who should build the new city and become its ruler.

Remus came back first. 'The gods chose me,' he said. 'Six magnificent vultures appeared to me and took flight. That was surely the sign.'

The Romans believed that Romulus and Remus were the descendants of Aeneas and belonged to a very ancient race. Livy wrote that Romulus built Rome on 21 April 753 BCE. A festival called Parlia marked its foundation. Romulus ruled Rome for thirty-three years. He disappeared mysteriously at the age of fifty-four and it was widely believed that he became the god Quirinus, the protector of warriors and crops.

As people rejoiced, Romulus returned. 'I saw twelve vultures spread their wings and soar into the heavens. The gods want me to rule the new city.'

While people argued who was right, Romulus began his task.

'I will build the boundaries of my city first, to show that it is impregnable,' he said.

When Remus heard his brother's words, he mustered all his strength and leaped over the walls, shouting, 'That's what I think of your city and its boundaries!'

Enraged by Remus's act of mockery, Romulus attacked and killed him. Then he thundered at the gathered crowd, 'And so will perish anyone else who leaps over my walls.'

In the time that followed, Romulus built a strong and powerful city which became one of the most famous in the world. It was named Rome in his honour.

Numa Pompilius

This story is about the way the Roman laws of worship and citizenship were made by Numa Pompilius in 716 BCE. The story also tells us that Numa invented the calendar. When he found that the cycles of the sun were longer but more regular than those of the moon, he added a day to some months to make them even.

The Romans believed that the god Jupiter was the protector of Rome. He was often confused with Zeus, the supreme god of the Greeks, because like Zeus he was god of the sky, rain, thunder and lightning. But the Romans also worshipped Jupiter for his role as the protector of law, fairness and goodness.

ONE YEAR AFTER THE DEATH OF ROMULUS, THE ROMANS CHOSE THEIR NEW KING. He was Numa Pompilius, from the Sabine town of Cures.

'I shall ask the gods for a sign to see if I deserve to be the king of Rome,' Numa told his high priest.

The priest covered Numa's head with a scarf and began the ceremony. He seated Numa on a stone facing south and sat to the right of him. The priest pointed skywards with a crooked rod, knotted in the middle, then drew a circle with it.

With his hand on Numa's head, he said, 'Father Jupiter, this man, Numa Pompilius, wants your permission to be king of Rome. If he has your blessing, show us light. If not, let the sky grow dark.'

The crowd that had gathered to watch the ceremony waited in silence. Suddenly, there was the sound of mighty thunder. Lightning flashed across the heavens. Jupiter had sent his sign. The gathering burst into loud cheers. They had a king!

'Romulus led you to glory,' Numa said. 'Now it is time to make laws of citizenship and proper worship.'

Roman men had fought for so long that they had forgotten how to live in peace, without a spear in their right hand and a shield in their left. Numa told them that the goddess Egeria revealed new laws to him each night as he prayed.

Then Numa walked into the centre of Rome and closed the door of the god Janus's temple. He declared, 'When the door to the temple is closed, we are at peace. When it is open, we are at war.'

Later, Numa decided that the year would be divided into twelve months and that certain days of the year would be set aside for worship and rest. This was the beginning of public holidays as we know them today.

Janus was the oldest Roman god. He was famous for having two faces. Since the time he had helped defend Rome against the Sabine army, the door to his temple had been left open. By closing the door, Numa showed that the Romans did not need Janus's help because there would be no war.

Juno's Warning

This story is about historical events which took place in 384 BCE. The Gauls were Celtic people from northern Italy who attacked and took over much of Italy around Rome. Over the years, archaeologists have uncovered a great deal of evidence of their attack on the city.

ONE DAY A YOUNG ROMAN MAN, PONTIUS COMINUS, SKIMMED ALONG THE RIVER TIBER. He balanced on a strip of cork just large enough to stand on. He was bringing an urgent message to the Senate in Rome, asking for help against the Gauls who were threatening to attack the Capitoline Hill.

The strip of cork floated easily on the water. When the Tiber was calm, he stood on it, using his arms to remain balanced. When the waters were choppy,

making the cork bob and toss, he lay flat on his belly. At moments the waves were so frightening he thought his end had come and he prayed to the gods to let him complete his mission. At last, far in the distance, he spotted the Citadel of Rome standing on the Capitoline Hill.

Pontius crept through the Gaul barricades and scaled a craggy cliff to reach the Senate. The message was well received. The senators agreed to help defend Rome against the Gauls. Pontius retraced his steps through the Gaul barricades, armed with the good news.

The leader of the Gauls discovered Pontius's tracks and was furious.

'Get yourselves ready, men!' he commanded. 'Let's attack the Citadel of Rome and show the Romans who's best.'

As the stars began to light the sky, the Gaul leader nudged the man next to him, and he the man next to him, until all the men were up and armed and ready to go. Very quietly, they moved towards the Capitoline Hill where the Citadel stood, stopping at a cliff so steep that it had been left unguarded. The men secured themselves to the cliff face, each one attaching himself to the arm of the one below, to form a human rope. They worked in complete silence: not the clatter of a rock, nor the squawk or flutter of a bird gave away their movements. Even the sharp-eared dogs of the city heard nothing.

Very soon, the man at the head of the human rope could see the crest of the cliff directly above his head. 'We shall reach the cliff top in less than an hour,' he thought. 'Rome will be in our hands tonight.'

In the Citadel, the night silence was shattered. Marcus Manlius, the Consul of Rome, sat up in bed with a start. What was that terrible noise? He strode to the window, trying to place the sound. It was coming from the geese in the temple of Juno at Arx.

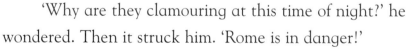

Juno, the wife of Jupiter and chief goddess, wears a goatskin and carries a spear and a shield. She is often seen with a peacock, her favourite bird. With Jupiter and Minerva, goddess of wisdom, Juno formed the Capitoline Triad. A temple was built to honour them in the Capitol, which was a religious and military centre in Rome.

'Why are they clamouring at this time of night?' he wondered. Then it struck him. 'Rome is in danger!'

Instantly, he took up his weapons and called his men to arms. Within moments, they covered the cliffs around the city and found the human rope woven by the bodies of the Gauls. Rushing to the cliff edge, Marcus struck the Gaul leader hard. The man lost his grip and toppled, taking his companions with him.

When morning came, the people of Rome heard what had happened and brought gifts for the soldiers.

'The goddess Juno protected us last night,' Marcus told them. 'We must thank her.'

And to remember that Marcus Manlius had saved Rome, the people of Rome named him Marcus Capitolinus after the Capitoline Hill.

Glossary

Aeneid – an epic poem in twelve volumes which describes the voyages of Aeneas, a Trojan prince, after the fall of Troy. It was written by the famous Roman poet Virgil.

Archaeologist – someone who studies the past by looking at the remains of ancient cultures.

Aventine Hill – one of the seven hills around Rome, found to the south of the city.

Capitoline Hill – also known as the Capitol, this was the smallest but most sacred of the hills surrounding Rome. It was home to the Citadel (fort) as well as the temple of Jupiter which was the most revered of all the temples in Rome.

Citizenship – the word used to describe being a citizen or inhabitant of a place. Citizens are thought to have certain rights and duties.

Consul of Rome – one of two magistrates (legal officials) elected by the people of Rome to protect the city's laws.

Crete – a large, mountainous island off the Greek mainland.

diviner – a person who is able to foretell or predict future events.

Elysian Fields/Elysium – a beautiful part of the Underworld. Only those who were noble and had committed good deeds during their lives were allowed to live there.

Erythrae – an ancient city, found in what is now the Asian part of Turkey.

Forum – a large public square in ancient Rome which was an important centre for business and politics in the town. It was also the site of many famous and important religious buildings, including the temple of Vesta.

Gauls – a tribe of people from western Europe. They were fierce warriors and became sworn enemies of Rome, attacking the city many times over the years.

Harpies – a hideous group of mythological creatures, with the faces and bodies of women and wings and claws of birds

Hesperia – the name the ancient Greeks used to describe Italy.

impregnable – strong, unable to be broken into or conquered.

Janus – the Roman god of doorways. Like a door which can look both in and out, he is always shown with two faces looking in different directions. The month of January is named after him, as he is seen to have one face looking at the events of the past year, while the other looks forward to the new one. His temple in Rome showed whether or not the city was at war. In times of war, the door to his temple was open and in times of peace it was closed.

Juno – queen of the Roman gods and goddesses and wife of Jupiter. Juno was the patron goddess of women, marriage and childbirth. In Greek mythology, she was known as Hera.

Jupiter – king of the Roman gods. He was worshipped by the Romans as the protector of their city and as the god of law and order. He was also known as the god of the sky and weather. In Greek mythology, he was known as Zeus.

Lavinium – the settlement founded by Aeneas which, over time, became the city of Rome. It was named after Aeneas's wife, Lavinia.

Mars – the Roman god of war and father of Romulus and Remus. In Greek mythology, he was known as Ares.

Mythology – the collection or study of myths.

Neptune – the Roman god of the sea. In Greek mythology, he was known as Poseidon.

Oracle – a priest or priestess through whom the gods were believed to speak. People consulted them to ask questions about the future, and the answers could come in the voice of a god or in a dream.

Palatine Hill – one of the seven hills that surrounded Rome. The Palatine is believed to be the site where the city was first founded by Romulus. It became the most important of the seven hills when later leaders of Rome built their palaces on and around it. The Forum was also found close to the hill.

Romulus and Remus – twin brothers who were the sons of Rea Silva, daughter of the king of Alba Longa, and the god Mars. In a fight over building a new city, Romulus killed his brother and founded Rome alone. The city took its name from him and he ruled over it for more than thirty years.

Senate – the government of Rome. Its members looked after matters of state, laws and religion.

Sibyl of Cumae – the most famous oracle or prophetess in ancient Rome, who lived in a cave in Cumae for nine hundred and ninety years. She foresaw the future of Rome and wrote her predictions down in books called the Sibylline Prophecies. These were kept in Jupiter's temple in Rome, where priests consulted them for advice and guidance. Some books say that the Sibyl of Cumae and the Sibyl of Erythrae were two different oracles, whose stories became confused over the years.

Thrace – an ancient part of south-eastern Europe, divided between Greece and Turkey.

Tiber – a great river which flows across Italy and through Rome.

Troy – an ancient city, found in what is now the Asian part of Turkey

Underworld – the world of the dead, where people go after they have died in the human world.

Venus – the Roman goddess of love. In Greek mythology, she was known as Aphrodite.

Vesta – the Roman goddess of the home and hearth or fireplace.

Vestal virgins – priestesses who served in the temple of Vesta. Their duties included tending a flame in her temple which was never allowed to go out.

Index